My First Book about

Meerkats

Amazing Animal Books

Children's Picture Books

By Molly Davidson

Mendon Cottage Books

JD-Biz Publishing

Download Free Books!

http://MendonCottageBooks.com

Read More Amazing Animal Books

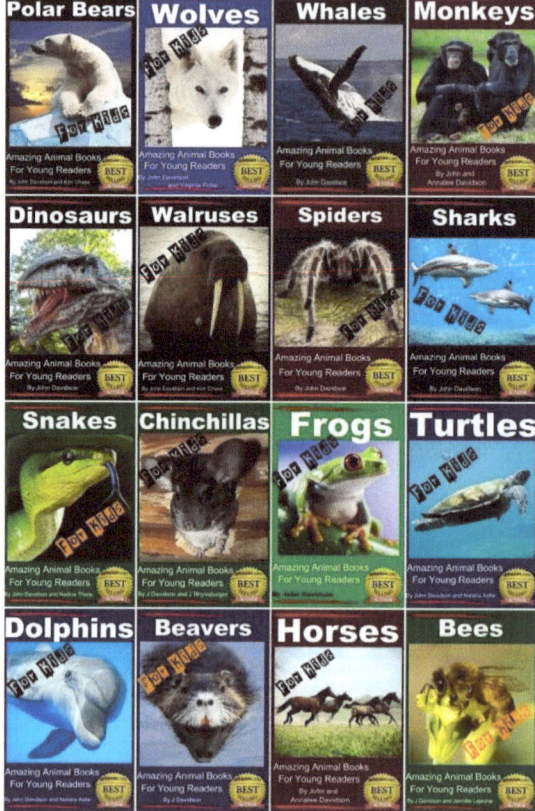

Purchase at Amazon.com

Download Free Books!

http://MendonCottageBooks.com

Table of Contents

Meerkat Facts

Meerkats are mammals; they have hair (not fur), breathe through their lungs, and give birth to live babies (they do not lay eggs).

A group of meerkats is called a mob, gang, or clan.

The word meerkat means "lake cat," but they are not cats, they are a mongoose.

What do Meerkats Look Like?

Meerkats only weigh about 1.6 pounds, and stand about 10 inches tall.

Meerkats will put their ears against the ground to listen for food. They can also close their ears, so when they are digging with their claws, dirt won't get inside.

They have long, pointy tails that help them balance when standing and also help them talk.

They all have different black patches around their eyes; this helps them find each other.

Where Do Meerkats Live

They live in hot, dry deserts; in Angola, South
Africa, Nambia, and Botswana.

Meerkats will dig underground to find water.

The desert temperature changes from 158°F (70°C)
in the summer to 14°F (-10°C) in the winter.

The Meerkat Home

They live in burrows, which are made by digging long, connecting tunnels underground, with many entrances on top of the ground.

Meerkats will sleep inside at night and go hunting for food during the day.

Large mounds of dirt, from digging the tunnels, is made around the burrow entrances, they use these to stand on to look for danger.

Sometimes, if they run out of food in an area, or another group takes control, they must build a new burrow, which is a long, hard job.

What Do Meerkats Eat?

Meerkats like to eat scorpions, snakes, spiders, eggs, and plants.

They do not store food in their bodies, so they spend most of their day eating.

To find food, meerkats will work in groups to forage, or dig, for food underground.

They will also always have one meerkat on the lookout for danger; if they sense danger they will bark loudly to warn the others.

What Animals Eat Meerkats?

Martial eagles like to swoop down and snatch up adult meerkats.

Meerkats are a jackal's, a small wolf, favorite food.

Cobras will try to strike and kill baby meerkats, the adults are too quick.

The Meerkat Mob

Meerkats live in groups, called mobs, with up to 30 others.

They are very loving toward each other; they will clean and stroke each other, especially if they haven't seen each other in a while.

In the group there will be one alpha dad and mom, who are in charge.

Meerkats are very playful, even the adults, they greatly enjoy wrestling with each other.

Different meerkat mobs may get into fights over territory since the land is where they get their food.

When mobs fight, they will jump on each other's backs while scratching and biting.

The alpha dads decide who has won, by whoever is still there after the fight, one mob will always retreat when too many get hurt.

Sometimes meerkat mobs will break up for a few reasons, if the alpha dad or mom die, if no new babies are being born, or if too many meerkats have died, because of disease, predators, or drought.

The Meerkat Family

Meerkats can have pups, babies, anytime of the year.

The pups will be inside the mother for 11 weeks before they are born; she usually has 4 - 5 each time.

The whole group will help take care of the pups; all the girls can feed the babies milk, even if they have never had babies.

A meerkat babysitter may die protecting the pups, if there is danger and they are unable to reach the burrow, the babysitter will lay on top the babies.

Only the alpha mom and dad can have pups, if other members do, the babies will be killed.

Meerkats Life Cycle

Meerkats are born blind, deaf, and with little hair.

When they are about 2 weeks old, they can start to see and hear.

They come out of the burrow, with a babysitter, at 3 weeks old.

When they reach a month old, a pup tutor teaches them how to start foraging for food.

The pups will stop drinking milk around 6 weeks, and start eating the same food as the adults.

For the next year, they will learn from others everything they need to know to be a successful adult meerkat.

When the pup turns one, it is considered an adult, it will start babysitting, being the lookout, and can start having babies.

Meerkats live between 6 - 8 years in the wild.

How do meerkats speak to each other?

They make many noises, they bark, growl, trill, and chirp.

One of the main reasons they talk, is to warn each other of danger; they have to be specific so the mob knows what and where the danger is.

Sometimes the danger maybe so close the meerkats don't have time to get back to the burrow, so they must just crouch down to avoid being seen.

A day in the life of a meerkat

They wake up as soon as the sun rises.

A lookout will go out of the burrow first, then will signal to the others if all is safe.

They may spend a little time soaking up the sun to warm themselves from the cold desert night.

The alpha father and mother will then decide where the mob will go to forage for food for the day.

They make take several breaks during the day, but they make sure they're back in their burrows by sunset.

The last meerkat into the burrow is the lookout, this way he/she can be the first out in the morning.

Meerkat relatives

Meerkats are part of the mongoose family, along with bandids, Kousi Mansi, and the dwarf mongoose.

Most mongooses are active at night, or nocturnal, but the meerkat is not.

A Yellow Mongoose

Meerkats in Captivity

When meerkats live in captivity, usually zoos, their life is very different.

They do not have any danger, and they always have plenty of food.

Meerkats in a zoo cannot form different mobs, since there is not enough space and they don't talk as much as they do in the wild, since there's no danger.

They live longer, about 15 years, and have more babies than wild meerkats.

Did you know?

In African folklore, the meerkat, called the Sun Angel, protects the villagers from werewolves, called the moon devil.

They are super fast diggers, they can dig their full body weight in dirt, in under one minute!

There are certain beetles, which live in the meerkats burrows, which they will not eat. Many scientists believe this is because the beetle eats their poop.

Could I have a meerkat as a pet?

Meerkats need to live in groups, if you had one as a pet, it would get rather lonely.

They forage for food, so they may try to dig through your carpet to find food!

To mark their territory, a meerkat will urinate; this will make your house stink.

If a meerkat gets scared it will become aggressive, it may hurt you, a member of your family, or a guest.

In conclusion, meerkats are NOT good pets.

Read More Amazing Animal Books

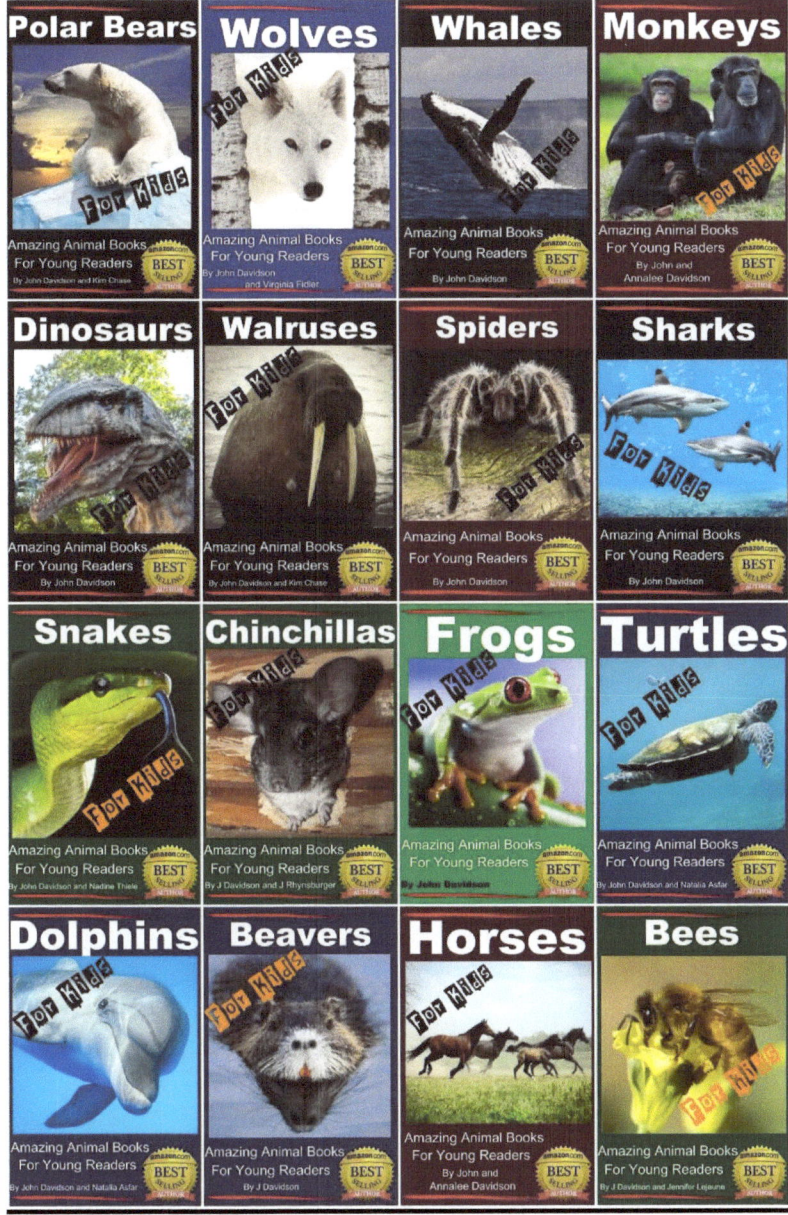

Purchase at Amazon.com

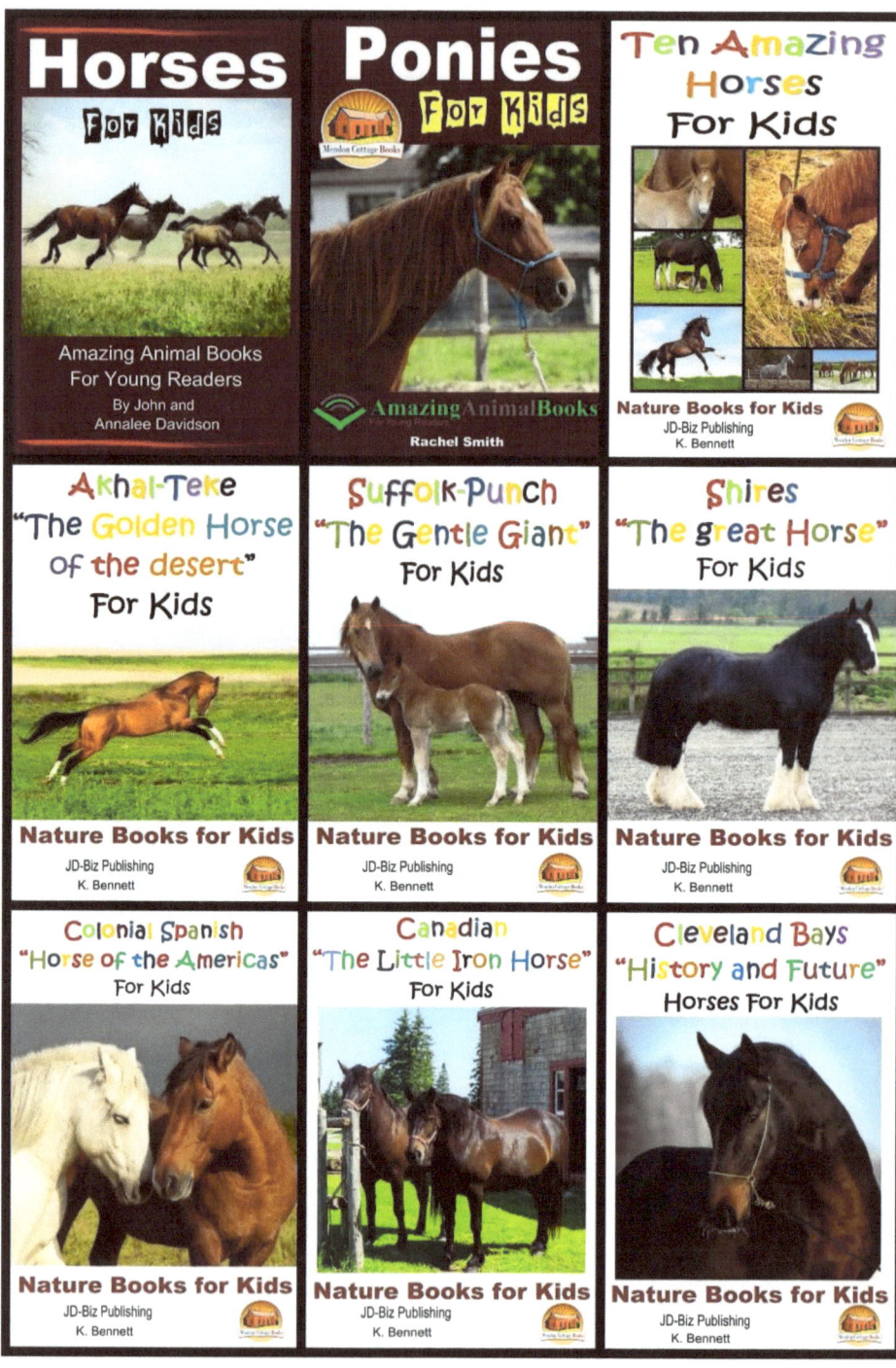

Our books are available at

1. Amazon.com
2. Barnes and Noble
3. Itunes
4. Kobo
5. Smashwords
6. Google Play Books

Download Free Books!

http://MendonCottageBooks.com

Publisher

JD-Biz Corp

P O Box 374

Mendon, Utah 84325

http://www.jd-biz.com/

Mendon Cottage Books

P O Box 374, Mendon Utah 84325

Mendon Cottage Books